Workbook for James Clear's
Atomic Habits

Printed Exercises for Reflection,
Processing, and Practising the Lessons

 BIG ACTION BOOKS

BigActionBooks.com

Contents

Claim your free bonus

There's a free bonus waiting for you as thanks for picking up this workbook. We think you'll like it. Inside, you'll find a list of the most impactful self development books from this year, including:

- Top books for self-growth and mindfulness
- Top books for financial growth
- Top books for relationships (including yourself)
- Top books for productivity and "Getting Things Done"

We hope they provide a little inspiration for you - and perhaps some new discoveries.

To get your free bonus, scan the QR code below or visit BigActionBooks.com/bonus.

Scan to get your free bonus

Introduction

Don't Just Think About Creating Life-Changing Habits: Actually <u>do it</u>.

WHY THIS WORKBOOK?

You've read James Clear's fabulous book about how to establish life-changing habits 1% at a time. Now it's time to actually *practice* it - write; journal; put the lessons in motion.

This workbook was created as a **companion** to James Clear's "Atomic Habits". While reading the book, we found ourselves wishing for a place where we could write, process and practise the book's lessons in a concise way. The takeaways here are profound - but there isn't much space to actually write in the book itself. Instead, we found ourselves cobbling together notes and action points in various places - notebooks, journals, pieces of paper - all of which would eventually get lost, or at the very least, didn't help us in putting the lessons into practice. That's how this workbook was born.

HOW TO USE THIS WORKBOOK

This workbook is like a faithful friend to Atomic Habits. In it, you'll find exactly what's advertised: the key lessons from the book, summarised & formatted, with space to write.

- All key lessons from Atomic Habits, extracted into one single place
- Space to write under each exercise
- Lists, ruled lines and space for you to answer, journal and reflect
- Clearly organised and well-formatted so it's easy to follow

In each section, we've extracted the main premise of the action points, and then added space to respond and practise the lessons. This may come in the format of a table to fill in, space to free-write, or other exercise methods to provide space for reflection. You'll also notice the "Parts" and "Chapters" referenced in the book, so you can easily find the section if you need to look back on it for further context.

If you want to not only read about how to create and establish life-changing habits - but also put the lessons into practice - this workbook, as well as your own dedication, will help you do just that.

Enjoy, and thank you.
Let's dive in!

---

* Please note: This is an unofficial workbook companion for Atomic Habits to help motivated do-ers process the lessons from this fantastic book. It is not created by or associated with James Clear in any official way.

Chapter 1: The Surprising Power of Small Habits

What Incremental Improvements Could You Make In Key Areas In Your Life?

Recall the book's example of the United Kingdom's cycling team having incredible success in improving thie results, by making dozens of '1%', small, incremental changes. **Where could you apply this to your own life?**

To start off, identity some areas you'd like to improve. These could be related to work, fitness, health, hobbies, family, relationships, income, etc <u>We suggest focusing on a maximum of 3-5 habits or areas for now</u>, rather than trying to optimize everything at once. You can always return to this process later to repeat the steps with other areas, if you'd like. Start small.

What are some small, incremental changes you could start making quickly, and stick to?

> **Note:** Throughought this workbook, you'll see examples in some places, listed in *grey handwriting like this*. These are just to give you an idea of the kind of action points you might like to take - but feel free to use or ignore them as best suits your style.There are also notes pages at the back of this workbook for journaling and free-writing.

Area	Incremental changes I could make
Health	→ *Go to bed 20 minutes earlier each night, to get more sleep.* → *Start a meditation practice - 2 minutes per day - after coffee.*
Finances	→ *Wait 24 hours before proceeding with any impulse purchase over $100.* → *Put aside an additional $X per week towards my savings.*

Turning Goals Into Habits

Recall the book's approach that habits are more important than goals. Goals are one-off targets, whereas habits create the systems that allow us to work towards those goals. For example:

Basketball Team:
- Goal: Winning a championship. (But every single team has this goal; so setting the goal itself isn't the answer).
- Habit: Daily training. Exercise. Shooting practice. Nutrition. Strategy. Etc.

We'll expand on this later in the workbook -- this exercise is just a starting point. What are some current goals on your radar, for which you could create habits as systems to improve your chances of success?

Goal	Habits I could create, as a system towards this goal
Finish marathon in December	→ Join a running club and run once per week with them → Run 4 x per week on Monday, Wednesday, Friday, Saturday
Increase revenue by 10%	→ Spend 30 minutes each day from 10-10.30am contacting potential new clients

Chapter 2: How Our Habits Shape Our Identity

Habits You'd Like To Change

Reflecting on the importance of habits in creating our identity (and vice versa), what are some current habits you would like to change?

For now we're not concerned with *how* we'll do that -- yet -- but just looking to identify them.

Habit I'd like to change	<u>Why</u> I'd like to change it
Snacking too regularly	→ *Disrupts my health routine, which is otherwise on-track*
Biting my nails	→ *I don't like the way it looks; can cause long-term damage to my teeth; not a nice habit.*

Identities You'd Like To Create

In the book, James Clear talks about how closely our habits are linked to our identity. And that, by creating a new identity, we can begin to cast 'votes' for that identity, which over time helps us concretize and truly believe that this identity is real.

Recall the example James gives of two smokers who are offered a cigarette, while trying to stop smoking:
→ *"No thanks, I'm trying to quit"*. This person still <u>identifies</u> as a <u>smoker</u>, even though they are making a concerted effort to stop smoking.
→ *"No thanks - I don't smoke"*. This person has <u>already begun identifying</u> as a non-smoker. They believe (or are starting to believe!) that they <u>are</u> a non-smoker. This is a powerful distinction that can help us create a new habit that benefits us.

Recall also the example in the book of James Clear's friend who lost 100 pounds by continually asking herself: *"What would a healthy person do?"*. She began to <u>identify</u> as a healthy person, making the choice to walk instead of drive, eating healthy, and so-on.

With this in mind: Using the table below, complete the following steps:
1. What identity (or identities) would you like to <u>create</u> for yourself (if they're new), or <u>continue</u> identifying as (if you do them already)?
2. Why is this important?
3. How can you cast 'votes' for this identity? Recall in the book that we start to <u>form</u> our desired identity by casting 'votes' in the form of actions. If I want to be a person who is invested in my own fitness, I cast a vote for that every time I go to the gym. If I want to be financially savvy, I cast a vote for that every time I save a dollar.

Example:

I would like to identify as this kind of person:	Step 1: This is important because…	Step 2: I can vote for this by…
→ Healthy - physical and mental	I want to feel energetic, look after myself, and be of service to others.	Walk instead of drive where possible. Complete my gym training.
→ Patient	With my friends and family - a good listener and able to talk and think in a calm way.	Make a conscious effort to ask probing questions. Really listen. Allocate enough time to hear.
→ Fun and adventurous	Adventure and fun are some of my key values and get me excited.	Discover a new place once per month (could be a day trip).

Your turn: What identity (or identities) would you like to <u>create</u> for yourself (if they're new), or <u>continue</u> identifying as (if you do them already)?

I would like to identify as this kind of person:	Step 1: This is important because...	Step 2: I can vote for this by...

Recognizing Negative Beliefs About Yourself

What kind of negative beliefs do you hold about yourself? For now, we're simply looking to identify them. Not to fix them, or to judge them, or to act on them. Recall some examples from the book:

→ *"I'm a nailbiter"*. This person was able to change this habit after identifying it.

→ *"I'm not good with directions"*. This kind of 'pigeonholing' is very common and easy to do. But bringing awareness to the fact that we sometimes create such negative identities for ourselves, is a big step towards overcoming and changing them.

With this in mind: What negative identities or traits have you created for yourself? What do you sometimes tell yourself, that you might like to change?

Negative identity	Notes (optional)
→ *"I'm not a morning person"*	
→ *"I'm not good with directions"*	
→ *"I can't remember peoples' names easily"*	

Chapter 3: Four Steps to Building Better Habits

Recap of the Four Laws

Recall the four laws of behavioural change: How to create good habits, and their inverse of how to curb bad habits:

Creating Positive Habits	Curbing Negative Habits
Make it <u>obvious</u>	Make it invisible
Make it <u>attractive</u>	Make it unattractive
Make it <u>easy</u>	Make it difficult
Make it <u>satisfying</u>	Make it dissatisfying

.. and the four steps involved in the habit feedback loop:
Cue → Craving → Response → Reward.

Thinking about 3 or more of the habits you'd like to develop, from the section above titled "Turning Goals Into Habits": How could you make the actions more obvious, more attractive, easier, or more satisfying?

Goal	Habits I'd like to Create	How could I make this obvious, attractive, easy, satisfying?
Finish marathon in December	→ Join a running club and run once per week with them → Run 4 x per week on Monday, Wednesday, Friday, Saturday	→ Add running club meetings to my calendar (obvious) → Go out for breakfast with the group after running (attractive) → Lay out my running clothes the nigh tbefore (easy) → Update my co-runners when I finish a session (satisfying)
Increase revenue by 10%	→ Spend 30 minutes each day from 10-10.30am contacting potential new clients	→ Put client list on my desktop (obvious) → Sit somewhere comfortable while talking on the phone (attractive) → Have all client details / contacts in one place (easy) → Drink my morning coffee after calls (satisfying)

Implementing the 4 Laws Into Your Own Habits

Your turn: How could you make the habits you identified earlier, obvious, attractive, easy, satisfying?

Note: You don't need to make <u>all</u> habits have each of these traits, necessarily. It must just be one: Making meditation easy. Making exercise satisfying. Etc.

Goal	Habit	How could I make this obvious, attractive, easy, satisfying?

Chapter 4: Habit Awareness (Or: The Man Who Didn't Look Right)

Become Aware of Your Habits: Create a Habits Scorecard

One important step to changing or creating habits is to identify them. With this in mind, use the book's "Habits Scorecard" method to create a judgement-free representation of your habits as they are <u>right now</u>. Do this by listing out your regular habits, with a note for positive, neautral or negative*:

+ positive LONG TERM

= neutral

- negative LONG TERM

* Note: When we talk about positive or negative habits, we are thinking <u>long term</u>. For example, smoking one cigarette (once) makes no difference. But smoking cigarettes every day, of course, has a very negative afffect on health in the long term.

List out your habits, either as individual habits (if you'd like to focus on a select few), or in areas such as a morning routinte as discussed in the book:

Habit or area of habits	Positive, neutral, or negative?
Morning routine (AREA)	= Wake up + Take 10 deep breaths - Check my phone for messages; reply if there are any = Take a shower + Do 20 push-ups
Smoking (HABIT)	- Smoking is negative to my health in the long-term
Weekly taco night (HABIT)	+ Positive: dedicated family time makes me feel happy and connected

Your turn: List out your habits, either as individual habits (if you'd like to focus on a select few), or in areas such as a morning routinte as discussed in the book:

Habit or area of habits	Positive, neutral, or negative?

Pointing And Calling: Bringing Habits To The Surface

Recall the 'pointing and calling' technique from the book, where Japanese train drivers reduced mistakes significantly - and even saved lives! - by pointing and calling, to draw attention to the steps involved in the work. This was a habit they intentionally developed, to improve their awareness and adherence to their commitment to their work.

Are there any areas you'd like to implement this technique in your life, pointing and calling - either pointing only, or, adding the vocal queue?

Area	How might I use pointing and calling?
I often forget my wallet when leaving the house	Point and call "Phone, Keys, Wallet" before stepping out of the front door
Snacking too much	Actively say to myself, "I am going ot eat another snack. Do I really want this right now?"

Chapter 5: The Best Ways To Build New Habits

Building New Habits: Implementation Intention

One of the most effective ways to build new habits is by setting written intentions. In Atomic Habits this is referred to as setting "Implemtnation Intentions". This involves actively writing down the habits you want to create, in concrete actions rather than abstract concepts.

These follow the formula: I will [BEHAVIOUR] at [TIME] in [LOCATION]

- Rather than: *"I want to work out more"*
- You might write down: "I will work out for 20 minutes on Mondays, Wednesdays and Fridays at 8am in my home gym".

After doing this for some time, it's common that at that time -- 8am in our example above -- your brain will <u>automatically</u> start thinking it's time to go to your home gym.

Set your own implementation intention(s) similar to the example below:

Formula: I will [BEHAVIOUR] at [TIME] in [LOCATION]

Behaviour ("I will")	At ("Time")	In ("Location")
Work out for 20 minutes	8am on Mondays, Wedsnesdays, Fridays for the next 2 weeks.	My home gym.
Meditate for 5 minutes	Before going to bed, after the kids have gone to bed, each night	On the chair in my living room

Your turn: set your own implementation intention(s) using the table below:

Formula: I will [BEHAVIOUR] at [TIME] in [LOCATION]

Behaviour ("I will")	At ("Time")	In ("Location")

Habit Stacking: Overhaul Your Habits, Using What You Already Do

Identity a habit you already do - and 'pair' / 'stack' other habits on top of it.

They follow the formula: After [CURRENT HABIT] I will [NEW HABIT]. In other words: after this thing I'm <u>already</u> doing, I'll do this other thing I <u>want to create a habit for</u>.

Because of the brain's tendency to associate habits with preceding actions, we can use the cue → craving → response → reward feedback loop to our advantage, by 'stacking' desired habits on top of existing habits.

Consider your own implementation intention, below. What desired habits can you stack on top of already existing habits?

Existing Habit	Habit to "stack" onto this action
I pour my coffee each morning	I will meditate for one minute
I take off my work shoes	I will put on my workout gear (to go straight to the gym)
I wake up in the morning	I will spend 1 minute thinking about 3 things I cam grateful for, before I get out of bed.

Chapter 6: Environment Over Motivation

Designing your <u>environment</u> in a way that's conducive to the habits you want to form, is critical. Recall the example of researching placing bottled water in vending machines, and seeing a subsequent (and immediate) drop in unhealthy soda sales - even without any announcements or promotion whatsoever. The simple *availability* of bottle water in the *environment* made all the difference.

Environmental: Positive Habit Changes

What <u>environmental changes</u> could you make at your home, office or anywhere else you spend your time, to help you form your <u>desired</u> habits?

Habit	Environmental Change I Could Make
Drink more water daily	Place a water bottle in the kitchen and lounge room for easy access
Exercise more regularly	Place gym gear and shoes in an easy-to-access spot; have a towel and drink bottle in the car ready-to-go

Chapter 7: The Secrets Of Self Control

Environmental Changes

In a similar way to using our environment to form <u>positive</u> habits like we did above, we can use the environment to curb <u>negative</u> habits, too. What <u>environmental changes</u> could you make at your home, office or anywhere else you spend your time, to help you <u>curb negative</u> habits?

Habit	Environmental Change I Could Make
Stop eating junk food	*Don't buy cookies at the supermarket; or, if they're around, place them out of sight (e.g. bottom of pantry, not at eye level)*
Stop biting my nails	*Pay for a manicure to help you feel great about your new nails*

One Space, One Use

On a psychological level, having 'mixed-use spaces' can be to the detriment of our forming good habits. In other words: having one space that functions for multiple purposes, doesn't help our brain recognise what that space is designed for.

If your lounge room is both your work space and your relaxing space, you're more likely to feel stressed and unable to let go of work. If your bedroom is where you sleep but also do your finances, you may find it harder to get to sleep.

With this in mind, which spaces are 'mixed' for you right now, and what ideas come to mind for how you might streamline them to assist with forming your desired habits?

Space	Current use(s)	Adjustments to improve habits
Kitchen bench	Cooking dinner + working on my laptop.	To stop working at night time and improve relaxation, buy a desk to separate work and non-work time.
Bedroom	Sleeping, scrolling social media	To help getting to sleep, only look at social media on my phone in the lounge room (not the bedroom).

Make Cues for Negative Habits Invivsible

What cues could you optimize in your environment to make cues for habits you want to stop, invisible?

Habit/Issue	Environmental Change I Could Make
Watch less TV	Move my TV out of the bedroom and into the lounge room. Place the control next to the TV (not on the coffee table) so it's slightly more effort to turn on the TV.
Not being productive at work	Place my phone on silent in another room for the first 2 hours of each day, to free up time and headspace for deep work.

Chapter 8: Making Habits Irresistable

To increase the probability of a habit occurring, we need to make it attractive. Habits are associated with higher levels of dopamine. It's the *anticipation* of a reward - not the fulfillment itself - that gets us to take action. Next, we'll work on how we can use this to our advantage.

Temptation Bundling: Make Your Habits More Attractive

Recall the example from the book of a man who realised he was watching too much Netflix (habit he wanted to change) and wanted to exercise more (habit he wanted to add). He engineered his TV such that it would <u>only</u> play netflix if he was riding his connected exercise bike. Another way to think about this is linking a 'want' (Netflix) to a need (exercise).

What are some 'wants' that you already do, that you can link to a habit you want to start?

Want (E.g. Netflix)	Need (e.g. Exercise)	How can I link them?
Watch Netflix	Exercise	Only watch Netflix whilst exercising
Get a pedicure	Clear work emails	Clear work emails before/while getting a pedicure

Advanced: Habit Stacking + Temptation Bundling

Next, we're moving into advanced territory - stacking <u>two</u> earlier techniques together: habit stacking and temptation bundling. This can create a domino effect of habits, and help our brains to more easily associate 'wants' with 'after completing this want, I will do X habit'. Recall the example from the book:

- I <u>want</u> to check Facebook
- I <u>need</u> to do 10 push-ups

Habit stack + temptation bundling:

- After I pull out my phone (with the *intention* of looking at Facebook)
- I will do 10 pushups
- After I do 10 push-ups, I will actually look at Facebook.

In this way, the 'need' leads to the 'want'. After a while, the brain begins to associate checking Facebook, with doing 10 push-ups, making it easier to do over time.

How can you use this in your own life?

Want	Need	Habit stack + temptation bundle
Check Facebook	*Do 10 push-ups*	*When I pull out my phone... I will do 10 push-ups. After I do 10 push-ups, I will check Facebook.*

Chapter 9: The Role of Family and Friends in Shaping Your Habits

In the book, we learn that habit formation is much more likely to occur when you surround yourself with others for whom that habit is already normal. Shared identity reinforces your individual identity.

Groups To Research Or Join

What groups could you look into or join, that would naturally help you improve your desired habits?

Groups I could join:

Joing a running club with a weekly running group on Tuesday mornings (e.g.: running habit) .

Look into 1 x weekly meditation class with a group, to get suggestions and accountability (e.g.: meditation)

Emulating Those We Look Up To

Whenever we are unsure, we look to the group to help us understand how to act. These generally fall into one of three categories, as mentioned in the book:

- The close (family and friends)
- The many (the tribe)
- The powerful (those with status and prestige)

Who are some people or groups you look up to, whose habits you might like to emulate?

My brother-in-law who runs every day and eats a healthy diet   (e.g.: running habit)

My classmate who is always calm and relaxed, and able to bring peace to any situation (e.g.: meditation)

Chapter 10: How to Find and Fix The Cause of Your Bad Habits

Making hard habits attractive

Recall from the book, how simply <u>reframing</u> a difficult habit can help alter our psychology, making the habit easier, more attractive, and more enjoyable.

Examples from the book:
- Rather than "*I <u>have</u> to make another sales call*"
- Reframing to: "*I <u>get</u> to make another sales call*" (I have a job and people to call, aren't I fortunate?)

- The man in the wheelchair: "*I am not limited by my wheelchair, I am liberated by it - otherwise I would be at home unable to go outside*"

- Saving money <u>now</u>, leads to freedom in the <u>future</u>. "*While it's tricky right now because I'm buckling down, my future self will thank me.*"

- Rather than "*I <u>need</u> to go for a run*"
- Reframing to "*It's time to build endurance*"

- In meditation, each interruption gives us a chance to practice returning to the breath

See the following page for space to write about your own habits and tasks, and how they might be reframed to create a positive association.

What habits could you reframe into a positive stance?

Current stance on a habit or task	Reframed stance with a positive angle
"I keep losing focus in meditation"	*"Every time I lose focus, that is a chance to practice bringing my attention back to the breath"*
"I need to go for a run"	*"It's time to build endurance!"*

Chapter 11: Walk Slowly, But Never Backward

This chapter discusses additional keys in establishing good habits. Making good habits <u>easy</u> is a huge step towards making them sustainable in the longer term.

Motion Versus Action: Where Can You Convert Enertia Into Action?

Action versus motion is an important concept, in that:
- Action is when we take concrete, actual steps that contribute to a habit.
- Motion is when we do research, thinking, discussing, and other steps that may (or may not) be necessary in establishing that habit, but that do not <u>actually complete the habit</u>.
- We want to be careful of not being in 'motion' too much, instead of actually taking action.

For example:

Habit goal: Regular Exercise Routine	
Motion	Action (we want to focus here!)
Talking to a trainer about exercising	→ Completing a gym session
Reading diet books	→ Buying good food and eating healthy

One more example:

Habit goal: Regular Meditation Practice	
Motion	Action (we want to focus here!)
Reading articles about meditation	→ Setting up a quiet space to meditate
Discussing meditation with friends	→ Sitting down to meditate for 10 minutes

Motion makes us 'feel' like we are getting thing done. Action is what actually gets things done.

Your turn: Reflecting on your own habits and what you want to create -- **what are some areas where you're in 'motion'? Can you shift some of those into concrete 'actions' instead?**

Remember to be kind to yourself - the goal here is just to <u>identify</u> if/where you're in motion, and gently shift those areas across to a place of action instead.

Where are you currently in Motion VS Action?

Habit: _____	
Motion	**Action**
	→
	→
	→
	→

Habit: _____	
Motion	**Action**
	→
	→
	→
	→

Habit: _____

Motion	Action
	→
	→
	→
	→

Habit: _____

Motion	Action
	→
	→
	→
	→

Habit: _____

Motion	Action
	→
	→
	→
	→

Taking Action: "Get Your Reps In"

This section discusses the importance of continuously working at your habits - whether in a small or a big way. James defines this in other terms such as "turning up, even when it's hard", and "getting your reps in".

The *amount of time* you spend doing something is not as important as the *number of times* you execute it.

In which areas are you already making good progress, or have set a good foundation, but need to 'get more reps in'?

The goal here is to reassure yourself that you're on the right track towards making these actions and habits more automatic. Habit formation is based on frequency; not time itself.

Areas where I need to 'get more reps in':

I'm running twice per week, but feel tired afterwards. Could I run 3-4 times per week, 2 of which are a shorter distance?

I'm missing some meditation sessions because I've run out of time. Could I do 2 minutes in those instances, instead of 0 minutes?

Chapter 12: The Law of Least Effort

Love Your Future Self: Easy Habit Creation

We are motivated to do what's convenient. How can you make it <u>easy</u> to do the habits you want to form? How can you facilitate ease for your future self? For example:

- The night before, set out the utensils to make a healthy breakfast the next day.
- At night, set out your gym clothes for the following morning.
- Place an egg timer next to your dedicated meditation space, to make it easy to time your session without needing to be distracted by your phone or other people.

How can you facilitate ease for your 'future self' in this way?

_____

_____

_____

_____

_____

_____

_____

_____

_____

Create Friction To Reduce Bad Habits

The inverse of the above is <u>adding</u> friction to bad habits, to make them harder and less convenient.

- After watching TV, unplug it, making it less convenient to sit down and watch again.
- Place unhealthy food in the very back of your pantry, or at the bottom of the fridge.

How can you add friction for bad habits in this way?

Chapter 13: How to Stop Procrastinating by Using the Two-Minute Rule

The Two Minute Rule: Simplify to Succeed

Recall the 2 minute rule: when starting a new habit, do it for 2 minutes or less, to make the friction as small as possible. (Almost anything feels possible for two minutes). Reduce your new 'habit' down to the bare minimum parts, to make it easier to get going. For example:

- Tie your running shoes (30 seconds)
- Take out your yoga mat (1 minute)
- Open my book and read 2 pages (2 minutes)

This helps to form a 'gateway habit' which then leads into spending more time doing the actual habit, over time.

Recall the book's example of the man whose desired habit was to form a regular exercise routine. He went to the gym for only 5 minutes for 2 months (!), then eventually said to himself *"Well, I'm here anyway, I may as well do a full workout"*. The habit became automatic, and he mastered the art of showing up.

What 'gateway habits' that take less than 2 minutes could you start to implement, as a stepping stone to your longer or more in-depth habits?

_____

_____

_____

_____

_____

_____

Habit Shaping: Phases to Greatness

Reflecting on the habits above, recall the examples of a <u>phased</u> approach over time. For example, if your desired habit was to become an early riser:

- Phase 1: <u>Be home</u> by 10pm every night.
- Phase 2: Have all <u>devices off </u>by 10pm.
- Phase 3: Be <u>in bed</u> by 10pm.
- Phase 4: Turn the <u>lights off</u> by 10pm.
- Phase 5: <u>Wake up</u> at 6am.

Not everything needs to happen all at once, and in fact this can make the habit much harder to implement.

What 'phases' could you implement in this way, for 1-3 of your key desired habits?

Habit: _____	
Phase 1	→
Phase 2	→
Phase 3	→
Phase 4	→
Phase 5	→

Habit: _____	
Phase 1	→
Phase 2	→
Phase 3	→
Phase 4	→
Phase 5	→

Habit: _____

Phase 1	→
Phase 2	→
Phase 3	→
Phase 4	→
Phase 5	→

Habit: _____

Phase 1	→
Phase 2	→
Phase 3	→
Phase 4	→
Phase 5	→

Reflections / notes on the above:

_____

_____

_____

_____

_____

Chapter 14: How to Make Good Habits Inevitable and Bad Habits Impossible

Make Bad Habits Hard

Recall the example of the author Victor Hugo, who took the (perhaps rather extreme!) approach of hiding away all his clothes during a writing deadline, to force himself to stay inside, instead of entertaining, and finish his book. This created extraordinary results by making his undesired habits (going out late and entertaining, instead of working on his book), virtually impossible.

Locking his clothes away was what James Clear calls a <u>Commitment Device</u>.

A commitment device is a choice you make <u>now</u>, to control future actions. Examples:
- Leaving your wallet at home when you go out, to avoid buying unhealthy food
- Buying individual meals instead of in bulk, to avoid over-eating

What "Commitment Devices" would you like to implement to help with your own habit creation?

Automating Habits

Many bad habits, or blockers, can be automated, so we don't even need to think about them. Recall some examples from the book, such as:

- The entrepreneur who purchased cash registers, to make employees' stealing of cash virtually impossible
- Purchasing a water filter to make water taste better and therefore more appealing to improve hydration
- Purchasing a great mattress for comfort to improve sleep
- Installing blackout curtains to darken the room (again, for improved sleep)
- Unsubscribing from emails, setting your phone to silent, or deleting games, to improve work focus and reduce distractions.

What automations or one-off actions could you take in a similar way, to support your habits and reduce the need to think about them or rely on pure motivation?

Chapter 15: The Cardinal Rule of Behavior Change

The standout theme here is: What is rewarded, is repeated. What is punished, is avoided.

With this in mind, how can we reward ourselves for doing habits we <u>want</u> to repeat, and pubish or make difficult, those which hinder us?

This could come in the form of:
- Adding rewards to habits - they could be large or small
- Reinforce the coherence to good habits we want to cultivate
- Making the avoidance of a bad habit, visible - as a reward.

For example:
- If you're trying to reduce impulse shopping, and instead want to save towards a larger-ticket item like a leather jacket you've been wanting for some time -- set up a bank account and call it "Leather Jacket". Every time you avoid an impuse buy -- even a small one -- transfer that money into the Leather Jacket account so you can watch it grow. Once you hit the amount needed, purchase the leather jacket.

With this in mind, what reward systems can you set up, so that you feel <u>immediately successful</u> when sticking to a habit, even in a small way?

Habit	Reward
Reduce impulse buying	→ Set up 'Leather Jacket' account; save using the money I'd otherwise have spent
Exercise plan	→ Reward myself with a massage at the end of the week if I stick to all gym sessions
	→
	→
	→
	→
	→
	→
	→
	→

Chapter 16: How to Stick with Good Habits Every Day

Visual Markers

Using <u>visual markers</u> to reinforce your habit formation and progress, can be an extremely rewarding and effective strategy, as we saw in the book with:

- The salesman who used the 'paperclip strategy', moving one paperclip from his jar of 120, to the empty jar, each time he made a sales call. He soon rose to prominence as one of the most successful salesmen due to this strategy and visual confirmation of how many calls he had made that day (calling 120 people, daily).

With this in mind, systems can you create to <u>visually</u> reinforce your habits?

Habit	Reward
Make sales calls	→ Start with 2 jars. 1 empty, 1 with 120 papercliips. Move 1 to jar after each call.
Daily meditation	→ Buy a calendar; cross off each day meditated, with a pen in my favourite colour
	→
	→
	→
	→
	→
	→
	→
	→
	→
	→

Habit Trackers: "Don't Break The Chain"

Sticking to a 'streak' or a 'chain' helps you build on your desired habits. Recall how:
- Comedian Jerry Seinfeld keeps an active streak of writing one joke every day. He doesn't focus on the *quality* of the joke -- it doesn't need to be one *great* joke per day -- but rather, he just aims to keep the streak going, and eventually great jokes emerge.
- Athletes of stick to a streak of workouts - each time they adhere to their planned training schedule, this counts as a day continuing the streak.

The author outlines the key tenet of: "Never miss twice". Breaking a habit once is fine, is inevitable, and is okay. It will happen. But he aims to never miss a second time.

Missing one day is just a mishap, a break in the streak. But missing two days is a trend away from the habit we are trying to cultivate. It's important to show up even on the days when you don't feel like it, or you need to reduce the scope a little to keep momentum.

What 'chains' would you like to create for yourself?

Habit	Chain
Meditation	→ *Meditate Mondays, Wednesdays and Fridays for 10 minutes. Track this.*
Eat healthy	→ *5 days per week, no sweet treats. 2 days: 1 sweet treat is ok. Track this.*
	→
	→
	→
	→
	→
	→
	→
	→

Advanced: You can also combine the earlier concept of 'habit stacking', with the tracking mentioned above.

For example:
- After I make a sales call → I will move one paperclip from one jar to the other.
- After I meditate → I will mark this off on my calendar

What habits would you like to 'stack and track'?

After I do this...	I will track the habit by doing this...
After I finish a workout	→ *I will log the workout for my trainer*
	→
	→
	→
	→
	→
	→
	→
	→

Chapter 17: How an Accountability Partner Changes Everything

By adding an immediate cost to any bad habit - or a cost of *not* adhering to a desired good habit - we can drastically increase the chances we'll stick to the new habit.

Habit contracts and accountability partners are two ways of achiving this.

The Habit Contract

Just like when governments around the world implemented seatbelts as a social contract (as well as a financial one, due to fines of non-adherence) - we can create our own habit contracts to help ourselves move in the right direction. The *punishment* of not following through is often much more powerful than a reward of following through. We can use this to our advantage.

Recall the example from the book of Brian, who after the birth of his son, wanted to improve his eating and fitness. He created a contract between himself, his wife, and his trainer:

Objective: Brian's #1 objective for Q1 is to start eating correctly so he can look better, feel better and hit his long term goal of 200lbs at 10% body fat.

Method:
Phase 1 - Implement slow carb diet in Q1.
Phase 2 - Start a strict macro nutrient tracking program in Q2.
Phase 3 - Refine the details of eating and exercising ("optimize"), and maintain this in Q3.

Daily habits: Write down all food consumed. Weigh himself daily.

Punishment: If Brian misses either of these daily habits, he will have to dress in formal attired to go to work, and/or wear a hat of his rival football team. If he misses a day of logging food, he will give his trainer $200 (per day missed).

Result: Brian then signed the contract, along with his with and trainer who were there to support him and hold him accountable.

In this way, what kind of accountability partners and/or contracts could you create for yourself, to help you stick to your habits like Brian did? See the following pages →

HABIT:

Objective:

_____

_____

Method:

_____

_____

_____

Daily Habits:

_____

_____

_____

Punishment for non-adherence:

_____

_____

_____

Signature(s):

Name: _____ _____ _____

Sign: _____ _____ _____

          Person 1   Person 2   Person 3

HABIT:

Objective:

_____

_____

Method:

_____

_____

_____

Daily Habits:

_____

_____

_____

Punishment for non-adherence:

_____

_____

_____

Signature(s):

Name: _____   _____   _____

Sign: _____   _____   _____

HABIT:

Objective:

_____

_____

Method:

_____

_____

_____

Daily Habits:

_____

_____

_____

Punishment for non-adherence:

_____

_____

_____

Signature(s):

Name: _____   _____   _____

Sign: _____   _____   _____

Chapter 18: The Truth About Talent (When Genes Matter and When They Don't)

Identifying our natural strengths can be a huge asset in habit creation and ultimately sticking with new habits.

Identifying your natural strengths

Note down some areas of natural 'strength' and enjoyment for you, using the following two points as a guide:

- What work is less painful for me than it is for others?
- What feels like fun to me, but work to others?

Your Skills In Combination

What combination of skills could make you stand out? Sometimes combining 1-3 of your existing skills can make you world-class at that specific combination.

Recall the example of the author of the Dilbert comics.
- He was not a world-class comic, but was **funnier** than the average person
- He was not a world-class artist (drawing), but **could draw** well
- He had some experience and skills in **business**
  → His **combination** of funny jokes and unique drawings, as well as his business acumen, helped him become world-class at that combination: drawing funny comics, and selling them to publications.

In a similar way, what **combination(s)** of skills and interests do you have, and how might they help you to create an area you can excel at?

Skill 1	Skill 2	Skill 3	Combination
Writing jokes	Drawing	Business	→ Selling funny comics to publications (Dilbert)
I speak French	Physics	Digital marketing	→ Create a French podcast about physics

Chapter 19: The Goldilocks Rule—How to Stay Motivated in Life and Work

Boredom is the enemy of progress. Keeping our habits exciting, and resetting expectations, helps us to stay on the edge of our comfort zone, and get into what James calles the Goldilocks Rule - in order to stay motivated in creating and sticking good habits:

- They need to be not too easy; not too difficult
- We need to feel <u>challenged</u> by them. Too easy, and we get bored. Too difficult, and we become disheartened to the point of wanting to give up.

Recall the example of the tennis match in the book: if you played against someone with much less skill than you, it would be too easy and you'd call the game off early. Play against Roger Federer, and you'd have no chance and become demoralized. What we want is a challenge that is approximately 4% harder than our current ability.

Use the table below to note down any habits/areas which might need more of a challenge to create the goldilocks effect.

In which areas / habits could you create a 'goldilocks' level of comfort? And how?

Habit / Area	Change to make ("How")
Meditation	→ 10 minutes has become too easy. Increase to 12, then 15, over two weeks, to challenge myself and go deeper.
Running	→ My 5KM running time of 25:00 feels easy now. Gradually decrease my target time by 30-60 seconds per session, over the next 2 months. 24:30; then aim for 24:00;, then 23:30; etc.

Chapter 20: The Downside of Creating Good Habits

Recall some regular habits the book recommends to regularly review and evaluate your progress:

December: Reflecting on the year just past.
- What went well?
- What didn't go well?
- What did you learn?
- For the author, he reflects on the business, new places visited, articles written.

Half yearly: Creating an 'integrity report', by asking questions such as:
- Am I living in line with my values?
- If not, what went wrong and how can I get back on track?

Identity Framing

The final exercise in the book discusses how we define our own identities. It's easy to fall into the trap of identifying as a particular <u>role</u>, such as "*I am a CEO*", "*I am a soldier*", or "*I am an athlete*".

But James reminds us that, inevitably, over time that <u>role</u> itself will change. Instead, we can create a more flexible identity, based on the <u>qualities</u> we contribute to that role. This means you can redefine yourself to keep important aspects of yourself, even if your identity changes. For example:
- I'm an athlete → I am mentally tough, and loves a physical challenge.
- I'm a great soldier → I am disciplined, reliable, and great on a team.
- I'm the CEO → I build and create things.

How can you create a more flexible identity, outside of your current role, such that you maintain your key qualities even if your role changes?

Role-Based Identity	Flexible Identity (based on <u>values/qualities</u>)
CEO	→ I build and create things, using my entrepreneurial spirit and lateral thinking to bring them into the world in an impactful way
Athlete	→ I am mentally tough, love to challenge myself and bring people together for physical improvement
	→
	→
	→
	→
	→

You made it!
You've completed the workbook.

Claim your free bonus

There's a free bonus waiting for you as thanks for picking up this workbook. We think you'll like it. Inside, you'll find a list of the most impactful self development books from this year, including:

- Top books for self-growth and mindfulness
- Top books for financial growth
- Top books for relationships (including yourself)
- Top books for productivity and "Getting Things Done"

We hope they provide a little inspiration for you - and perhaps some new discoveries.

To get your free bonus, scan the QR code below or visit BigActionBooks.com/bonus.

Scan to get your free bonus

Would you help us with a review?

If you enjoyed the workbook, we'd be so grateful you could help us out by leaving a review on Amazon (even a super short one!). Reviews help us so much - in spreading the word, in helping others decide if the workbook is right for them, and as feedback for our team.

If you'd like to give us any suggestions, need help with something, or to find more workbooks for other self-development books, please visit us at BigActionBooks.com.

Thank you

Thank you so much for picking up the Workbook for James Clear's *Atomic Habits*. We really hope you enjoyed it, and that it helped you practise the lessons in everyday life.

Thanks again,
The Big Action Books team

Notes:

Notes:

Notes:

Notes:

_____

_____

_____

_____

_____

_____

_____

_____

_____

_____

_____

_____

_____

_____

_____

_____

_____

Notes:

Notes:

Notes:

Made in United States
Orlando, FL
21 March 2024

45008812R00035